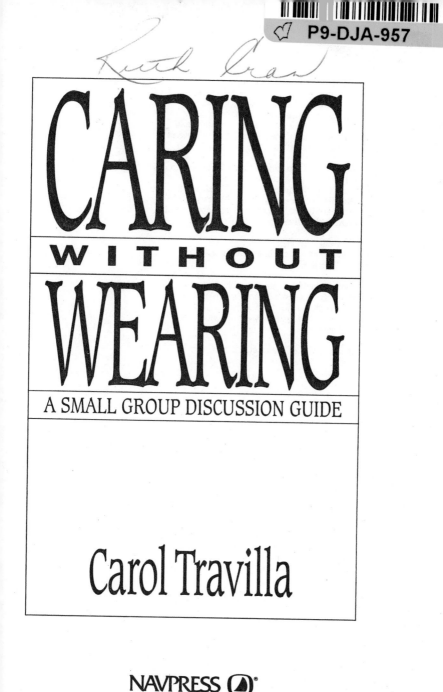

CARING

WITHOUT

WEARING

A SMALL GROUP DISCUSSION GUIDE

Carol Travilla

NAVPRESS
A MINISTRY OF THE NAVIGATORS
P.O. BOX 6000, COLORADO SPRINGS, COLORADO 80934

The Navigators is an international Christian
organization. Jesus Christ gave His followers
the Great Commission to go and make disciples
(Matthew 28:19). The aim of The Navigators is to
help fulfill that commission by multiplying laborers
for Christ in every nation.

NavPress is the publishing ministry of The Navigators. NavPress publications are tools to help
Christians grow. Although publications alone cannot make disciples or change lives, they can help
believers learn biblical discipleship, and apply what
they learn to their lives and ministries.

Printed in the United States of America

Contents

To my husband, Ken,
who has taught me the most about caring
by the way he has cared for me.

Author

Carol Travilla is a licensed psychologist and marriage and family therapist, currently practicing in Minnetonka, Minnesota. Her background includes teaching, personnel work, and directing the Christian education program of a large church in Michigan.

For more than twenty-five years Carol has been a pastor's wife. She and her husband, Ken, live in Eden Prairie, Minnesota, where he is an associate pastor at Wooddale Church. They have two adult children.

Ken and Carol teach seminars on *Caring Without Wearing*.

Acknowledgments

Special thanks to Dorothy Dahlman who sparked the idea for the one-day seminar, Bob Putman who tutored me through this project, my children who encouraged computer confidence, my prayer-support group and the many friends who expressed care by faithfully praying for me.

Preface

Caring for one another is at the heart of Christianity. The Scriptures are filled with admonitions to encourage, be present with, and meet the needs of those around us.

From my experience of giving and receiving care, I recognize that it is possible to have intense desire and to know all about the approaches to caregiving, but to experience times of frustration and burnout. When this happens, the caregiver is limited in his or her ability to care for others.

This study guide is designed to help participants explore what the Scriptures teach about caring for others and for themselves. It is not a book about counseling but about caring and support. The first four sessions deal with the many ways to express understanding and acceptance to hurting people.

Self-care as the key to avoiding burnout is the theme of the later sessions. We must be sensitive to what we can and cannot do. Caring too much, feeling the need to change another person, and having unrealistic expectations get in the way of providing care that is helpful.

As you meet in groups to use this guide together, I pray that you will be able to give and receive love and concern for one another. Then, as you receive care, you will be able to reach out and give care to that neighbor or loved one who needs you, thereby fulfilling in all its facets our Lord's command to "love one another as I have loved you" (see John 13:34).

You can also use this guide on your own. However, you will gain a great deal more if you share your answers with at least one other person.

Caring

What Does a Hurting Person Really Need?

I drove into the visitors' parking lot of the state mental hospital still stunned with disbelief that I was there to visit my dad. As a bride of twenty-one, I could remember the joy in his face as he had walked me down the aisle just nine months earlier.

Our wedding pictures resembled those of the perfect "pillar of the church" family. We were Focus on the Family personified. But the smiling faces in the pictures mocked the reality. No one prepared me for a personal encounter with mental illness and emotional breakdown. Those words were foreign to me.

The shock that my father did not recognize me brought uncontainable tears. I thought my heart would break. I turned to my faith and to my friends for comfort and an explanation.

But there were no pat answers that would bring me instant relief. There were no easy solutions to ease my hurt or compensate for the loss. There was no quick fix for my father or our family. I discovered that my task was to find the strength and wisdom to live through one day at a time. It was my first experience of loss, suffering, and intense pain.

Since my father and mother held leadership roles in the church, our family received much love and concern. However,

I still wince when I remember the "help" that was not helpful. Help that felt impatient or judgmental never comforted us. Insinuations that lack of faith or disobedience had gotten us into the situation or inferences that someone else knew *exactly* how we were feeling only added to our pain.

Little did I know how much care I would need through the years. I've spend a good part of my adult life sorting out why bad things happen to good people. I have needed care not only in times of crisis but also in transition times when I've had to adjust to change. This book is written out of my experiences with the many people who listened to me, supported me, allowed me to struggle and make right and wrong choices, but never withdrew their belief in me through my own healing and growing. It also comes from years of experience as a psychologist listening to others report gestures of care that were both helpful and hurtful. I want to pass along what the caregivers in my life have taught me about help that is helpful. I want to help you show care to others in ways that bring hope and comfort to them without hurting you.

WHAT IS CARING?

At some time in our lives, we all need care. Caring that makes a difference begins with compassion, understanding, and acceptance. In other words, *caring is responding in helpful ways to hurting and nonhurting persons.*

1. Begin your time together as a group by getting acquainted. On your own, complete the following sentences. (If you have no answer for one of them, skip it.)

   a. One thing my mother nagged me (or should have nagged me) about when I was a kid was . . .

   b. I heard about this group through . . .

   c. One thing I would like you to know about me is . . .

2. Now pair up; if there is an uneven number of people in the group, one "pair" can include three people. Share your name and your answers to question 1 with your partner(s). Listen well because you will introduce your partner to the group in a moment.

3. Reassemble in the larger group. Go around the group, each person introducing his or her partner by giving the name and one thing learned about the partner.

    The focus of our first session will be to *identify caring gestures* that are helpful to people needing care. We will also look at *characteristics of hurting people* so we can develop a sensitivity to the needs of others.

4. Think of a time when you needed care and wanted someone to help. What did you need?

People who need care are usually. . .

 ◆ Experiencing a loss.
 ◆ Feeling uncertain about the future.
 ◆ Requiring comfort.
 ◆ Wanting understanding and acceptance.
 ◆ Looking for hope.

5. a. Does the list above include what you were going through? If so, which item(s)?

   b. If not, how was your situation different?

6. Briefly describe the caring gestures that were helpful to you when someone responded to your need.

7. Develop a list of descriptive words about caring people (for example, gentle, willing to listen).

Stories about hurting people and the ones who helped them reveal that different hurts have varying impacts on lives and that some situations are resolved more easily than others.

There are times when a person needs only some direction or information. When I moved to a large city from a rural community hundreds of miles away, I needed information and new friends to give support and show me around. I was hurting, temporarily disoriented with the unfamiliar, and needed some assistance to find my way in a new city. In time, and with guidance from others, my comfort level increased.

But many life situations do not resolve with time and information. Most of our hurts are from ongoing situations, even though they may have begun with a crisis.

Consider these examples:

♦ The parents of a teenaged son involved in an automobile accident and left in a coma indefinitely.
♦ The father whose job is terminated because the company went bankrupt or was bought out.
♦ The unwed mother who wants to keep her child.
♦ The single parent who receives a medical diagnosis of an incurable disease.
♦ The widow without financial security.

These people are all experiencing a loss. They need comfort and are looking for hope. In the following sessions, you will learn more about the kind of help that helps when the people around you need understanding, acceptance, and the assurance that they are not alone in their struggles and pain.

THE BIBLE'S MOST FAMOUS UNWED MOTHER

8. Read Luke 1:26-42 to learn about a biblical person struggling with a situation that had no easy answer.

   a. What was Mary's crisis?

   b. How do you suppose she was feeling when she arrived at Elizabeth's house?

   c. What do you think she needed?

If your answer to the last question included the concepts that Mary needed *understanding* and *acceptance,* you are well on your way to recognizing the first principle of caring. Giving comfort and hope involves expressing understanding and acceptance through each stage of a person's struggle.

9. How did Elizabeth respond to Mary?

10. Read Luke 1:56. What do you imagine occurred during those three months?

LET'S GET PERSONAL

11. a. On your own, think about your family and friends in your immediate world. Write down the name of one person you know who is going through a life situation that has no easy solution.

    Name

    Situation

    b. In what ways can you show understanding and acceptance to this person in the coming week?

12. As a group, discuss the obstacles you might have to overcome in showing this care.

Close in prayer. First, tell the person on your *left* the name of the person you have chosen to care for in particular this week. (The person on your *right* will tell *you* someone's name.) Then take turns praying that God will enable the person on your *right* to minister to the person he or she named.

Why Should I Care?

When Susan came to see me at my office, she was suffering in several ways. It had been two years since her two-year-old daughter's death, and she was confused because her grief was still overwhelming. She was upset about conflict in her marriage, very bitter toward would-be helpers, and extremely impatient with herself.

As we spent several sessions exploring her feelings, her expectations of the healing process, and her relationship with friends, we uncovered Susan's fear and inability to ask anyone for help. I suggested she let a close relative know how she felt, so Susan wrote the following in a letter:

> I can't seem to move ahead because there is still a large, raw wound there. Mostly I feel as though I'm on an island way out in the ocean and no one knows I'm there. If they knew, they might try to get to me and help. But two things prevent this. Other people don't/can't understand the level of pain and loss this has brought so they don't venture into the water. And I seem to be unable to attempt the swim myself. What if they don't throw me a rope when they see me coming? What if I make it and they don't understand how difficult the trip has been? I guess I am desperate for someone to

really understand how my life, and how I look at it, is now forever changed.

1. a. Can you think of a time when you felt as if you were on an island with your pain and no one seemed to understand? What ropes did you need to help you swim to shore?

   b. If you have not experienced this, can you think of someone who may be feeling like Susan? What ropes could you throw to that person?

In this session we will continue to identify ways to carry out God's command to provide the help people need when walking through grief, uncertainty, loneliness, and pain. We will begin by examining what the Scriptures say about why we should express care to others.

WHAT THE BIBLE SAYS ABOUT CARING

Giving and receiving care are recurrent themes throughout the Bible. We are going to look at some reasons the Bible gives for showing care to others.

The group can divide into pairs or triads and choose one question (from 2 to 7) for each pair. Take five to ten minutes to research your answers.

2. *God commands His disciples to care for one another.*

   a. According to John 13:34-35, why does God give this command?

b. How does Jesus describe care in this passage?

3. Read Deuteronomy 10:18-19.

   a. Who are we commanded to care for and why?

   b. Who might be the "alien" in your church or community today?

4. *Caring for others is God's plan for meeting the needs of people.*

   a. How does Paul describe caring in Galatians 6:2,10?

   b. Give some practical examples of what Paul is getting at.

5. Read Luke 10:29-37.

   a. What were the needs of the man on the side of the road?

   b. How did the good Samaritan respond to those needs?

c. What are the needs today of the people around you?

6. *Caring is rewarding and fulfilling.*

    a. What kind of rewards do Matthew 10:42 and Galatians 6:9 refer to?

    b. Do you think there are present rewards for ministering to people? If so, what are they?

7. *Caring for others is the first step to evangelism.*

    a. Read 1 Thessalonians 2:7-8. How does Paul portray his ministry?

    b. In what ways can you share your "lives" with unbelievers so that you can share the gospel as well?

    c. Describe a present-day situation that is an example of this principle.

8. Get back together as a large group. Each pair or triad can report one or two key insights gained from the passages you examined.

MORE CARING GESTURES

Whether we desire to fulfill God's command to care, want to share Christ with someone, or endeavor to meet the needs of others, we may fear that we are not doing enough.

Take a moment to think about the ways you are already fulfilling this command and meeting the needs of others.

9. a. On your own, read the following checklist, and put a check mark next to every way you've expressed care to another person in the past six months.

Sending a card	Doing manual labor
Providing transportation	Holding a hand
Caring for a child	Extending hospitality
Preparing food	Making a hospital visit
Contributing financial help	Providing nursing care
Furnishing career assistance	Tutoring
Writing a note	Being present
Taking a meal	Offering prayer
Giving a hug	Cleaning
Listening actively	Discipling
Presenting a gift	Making phone calls
Shopping for food	Visiting a home
Volunteering	Sewing
Giving a party	Reading

   b. Next, complete the following sentence. As a result of doing this exercise, I realize that I usually throw ropes to hurting people by . . .

10. Now, as a group, discuss what you have discovered by doing this exercise.

11. In Ephesians 2:10 we read, "For we are God's workmanship, created in Christ Jesus to do good works, which God

prepared in advance for us to do." God not only prepares the works, He prepares us to do them.

a. Second Corinthians 1:3-4 tells one way He does this. What is that way?

b. How have you experienced yourself being prepared ahead of time to care for others in need?

An unknown author's poem may help you remember ways to care:

Sharing

There isn't much that I can do, but I can share my bread with you, and sometimes share a sorrow, too—as on our way we go.

There isn't much that I can do, but I can sit an hour with you, and I can share a joke with you, and sometimes share reverses, too—as on our way we go.

There isn't much that I can do, but I can share my flowers with you, and I can share my books with you, and sometimes share your burdens, too—as on our way we go.

There isn't much that I can do, but I can share my songs with you, and I can share my mirth with you, and sometimes come and laugh with you—as on our way we go.

There isn't much that I can do, but I can share my hopes with you, and I can share my fears with you, and sometimes shed some tears with you—as on our way we go.

There isn't much that I can do, but I can share my friends with you, and I can share my life with you, and oftentimes share a prayer with you—as on our way we go.[1]

THE HEALING POWER OF BEING THERE

As a visitor from another city, I listened closely while the members of a Sunday school class shared their concern for

Ralph, whose wife had just left him and their three young children. It immediately became evident to me that these people really wanted to care for other members of their class.

They were talking about what to do for him when Ralph walked into the class. One person asked him if she could provide some meals for the family. Others responded with various offers, endeavoring to help.

I felt a lump rise in my throat when Ralph looked at the class and said, "The food would be nice, but I really need someone to eat it with me."

How easy it is to minimize the power of presence when expressing help and acts of kindness to people in need!

12. Think of a specific time when someone comforted you by just being there. Two or three people may want to share their experiences briefly with the group.

    Martha Stout is correct in asserting,

    > We are not called to take away each other's fear or fill up each other's loneliness. . . . We're called instead to simply be present to each other, to be willing to stand with each other, in times of distress; perhaps offering a word or the touch of a hand, perhaps just sitting in silence.[2]

LET'S GET PERSONAL

13. Share with your group one thing you have become aware of during this session about your own needs or the way you care. Write down what the person on your left says.

14. Take a minute on your own to identify one act of love you would like to carry out with someone this week.

As you close, thank God for what He has taught the person on your left. If a need was expressed, ask Him to fill it. Close by asking the Lord to help you this week to fulfill His command to care and meet the needs of others.

Tips for Things You Can Do

Making Phone Calls. Make a practice of asking the person if it is a convenient time to call. Check out his or her comfort level at the time of the call. Keep the call brief. The person should *want* another call from you rather than fear it. Keep the focus of your call on the other person.

Sending Cards. Sending cards is a wonderful way of letting someone know that you are aware of the circumstances and want to empathize with his or her situation. Whether it is celebrating a great joy, sending a note of encouragement, or thanking him or her for a gift or service, sending a card is a universal, readily available way of sharing in someone's life. Cards can be read at a quiet time without interruptions. They can be enjoyed again and again and saved for times when one might feel alone or forgotten.

Be careful not to make comments in your notes that convey pat answers or easy solutions. Do not assume you know a person's spiritual condition. Do not assume you know how another person feels. A key ingredient in help that is helpful is to be sensitive to the hurting person's circumstances, checking out what he or she needs and showing a gentle kindness as you express love and concern.

Visiting. Sometimes "just being there" is even more powerful when you take a few minutes to invite God to be there with you and the hurting person. Prayer that focuses on who God is and what He is able to do can be a way of offering hope. Of course, we want to strenuously avoid prayer that is really a subtle way of telling God or the hurting person what to do. And it's always wise to ask the person, "May I pray with you?"

Your Most Valuable Caring Skill

When my daughter Karen was in the eighth grade, I was also going to school, learning about the communication skill called active listening. One morning I was up early packing lunches and getting the kids ready for school. Eighth graders are not always the happiest people in the world. They're delightful, but they are going through changes and need a lot of understanding in their struggles. Karen was no exception.

She came into the kitchen and started complaining, "I hate school; it's so cold there. The teachers are unfair. . . ." She went on and on.

We had enrolled her in a private Christian school and I immediately prepared to make a self-righteous response, such as, "You ought to be grateful you can go to that school. Do you know how much your father and I sacrifice so you can go there?" I was ready to give a mini-lecture about how blessed she was to have us as parents, how it was the most wonderful school in the whole world, and so on. Fortunately, before I said anything, I remembered what I had learned the night before. The instructor had said to *listen to the speaker's content but then focus on the underlying feeling in his or her words.* Many times the content is the smokescreen for what the person really wants to share about his or her feelings.

I mentally erased the content part about its being a

terrible school and switched to concentrate on Karen's feelings. I listened to her tone of voice and watched her body language. It was cold and tight. I turned to her and said, "Karen, you're feeling miserable this morning, aren't you?"

To my great surprise, she stopped in her tracks, turned around, went to her room and dressed, then ate breakfast and left for school without another word. I had acknowledged her feelings by my response and showed that I really was listening and that I really did care about her.

Many times since that morning I have found that if my heart attitude is to really listen to someone's feelings, I can respond with empathy.

As we continue exploring ways to be Jesus' disciples by showing care for others, our attention turns to the art of listening. As we progress through the next sessions, we will consider listening to others, listening to God, and listening to ourselves. Listening—*making a conscious effort to hear*—is essential to a helping relationship.

WHY IS IT IMPORTANT TO LISTEN?

The virtue of listening is that it conveys your concern for the other person. Jesus often took time to listen to people and respond to their needs. Before healing the daughter of the Canaanite woman, He listened to her testimony of faith (Matthew 15). He listened to Nicodemus's questions (John 3). He listened to Mary and Martha's grief over Lazarus's death (John 11), the questions of the rich young ruler (Mark 10), and the anguish of the men on the road to Emmaus (Luke 24).

Haddon Robinson, president of Denver Seminary, says, "If I were asked to choose the single most important skill for counselors, it would be the ability to listen. The only reason some people have a secret sorrow is that the rest of us won't take time to listen to them."[1]

Ann Landers, syndicated columnist to the lovelorn and the hurting, was keynote speaker at the National Convention of the American Association for Counseling Development. In her address she remarked, "The success of my column underscores for me one of the principal tragedies of our time: There are people out there who have no one to talk to."

Each of us needs to be understood and accepted. We need to be listened to without judgment.

1. Think of a time when you were relieved of a burden because someone simply listened to you. Share your story with the person next to you.

UNDERSTANDING ACTIVE LISTENING

Active listening requires that *we get inside the speaker,* that *we grasp from his or her point of view just what the person is communicating to us.* More than that, *we must then convey to the speaker that we are seeing things from his or her point of view.*

Active listening is listening intently to both verbal and nonverbal messages. For instance, let's say I'm listening to Paulette. Active listening means I will give her rapt attention and then convey to her that I see things from her perspective—*without making judgments or giving advice.* I hear out Paulette instead of interrupting and responding from my perspective.

There are two components to all messages. The first is the content—the facts or the words. The second is the feeling or attitude underlying the message. Both are important and both convey meaning. *Active listening is listening for total meaning.*

Most of us naturally respond to the content of what we hear, as I nearly did with Karen in the opening story. But until you really listen to what is going on, getting underneath the content to the underlying feeling, you don't know how to help. Think of how the Sunday school class (described in the last session) could have missed what Ralph really needed if they had not had the opportunity to listen actively to him.

Learning to listen actively to others will help you. . .

◆ Express empathy.
◆ Gather all of the facts rather than jump to conclusions.
◆ Provide a sounding board for the person to think through the issue and discern what to do.
◆ Avoid giving insensitive answers or unwise counsel.

So how do we learn to listen actively? By practicing.

2. For this question, your group can divide into triads. Each triad should choose one of the following situations. After reading the situation, *individually* do the following three things. Then share your answers with your partners.

◆ Underline the content (facts) of the message.
◆ From the words listed under "Feeling Words and Possible Openers for Active Listening" (page 37), choose ones that you think describe what the speaker is feeling and write them down.
◆ Write out a response that reflects what the speaker has just said. For example: It seems you are feeling
_____ because _____.

Situation A. Since my husband has retired, he expects me to be at home all the time. He doesn't like my going to Bible study or working at the food shelter. I don't know what to do.

Underline the content (facts).

What do you think the speaker is feeling?

Write out a reflective response.

Situation B. One of my friends has turned his back on me. We have been friends for a long time, but when I see him, he won't speak to me.

Underline the content (facts).

What do you think the speaker is feeling?

Write out a reflective response.

Situation C. I can hardly wait! My wife and I are going to Florida next week, and we have not been away for over two years.

Underline the content (facts).

What do you think the speaker is feeling? (Note that we share people's joys as well as their sorrow.)

Write out a reflective response.

Situation D. My son is failing in school. When I talk about it with my wife, she seems to act as if it doesn't matter to her.

Underline the content (facts).

What do you think the speaker is feeling?

Write out a reflective response.

Situation E. I just learned that my mother has cancer. She lives hundreds of miles from me.

Underline the content (facts).

What do you think the speaker is feeling?

Write out a reflective response.

3. Someone from each triad can read one of the triad's reflective responses to the whole group.

A COMMON MISTAKE

Giving advice or a pat answer immediately can result in the speaker feeling unheard, minimized, or misunderstood. The art of active listening involves giving your full attention to the speaker so that you grasp what he is communicating to you from his perspective. Responding in a caring manner requires staying with what the speaker has said and trying to convey to him that you are seeing things from his point of view. It is a way of clarifying what you have heard.

Perhaps it would be useful to think in terms of a tennis game. The server serves the ball and puts it in the opponent's court. A courteous player will focus on the serve and do all he can to return it rather than ignore the serve and hit his own ball. So it is with active listening. The key is staying with the other person and what he or she is experiencing.

4. In your triad, choose one person to be listener and the other two to be speakers. The first speaker should make a statement about anything he or she wants to talk about. (Keep it to a minimum of three sentences.) The listener will respond to the speaker with a reflective statement. Then the second speaker should make a statement, and the listener will respond reflectively. Then change roles until all three people have had a turn at being the listener. You may use the lists under "Feeling Words and Possible Openers for Active Listening" to identify feelings and openers for your active listening responses.

5. Now let's see how it works in actual conversation. You

meet Mary in the hallway at church and she tells you: "I love my job, but since Jamie was born, I can't seem to keep up. I don't like taking her to childcare, but Tim says we need my income to stay in our new home."

Consider how you would respond to Mary, remembering the following principles of active listening.

Listen to Mary's feelings.

Keep the focus on what Mary is saying, not on your need to "fix" her.

Do not give advice or be judgmental.

Write your response to her.

6. Three or four group members can take this opportunity to read their responses to Mary.

Now let's say that you are all masters at active listening. Two volunteers can role-play the following dialogue.

Mary: "I love my job, but since Jamie was born, I can't seem to keep up. I don't like taking her to childcare, but Tim says we need my income to stay in our new home."

You: "You seem to be feeling torn between working and staying at home."

Mary: "Yes. Every morning when I leave for work there are dirty dishes in the sink and laundry to be done. Those are the first things I see when I get home."

You: "You're really struggling with all you have to do."

Mary: "That's right, and I don't think Tim understands how hard this schedule is for me. I really want to be with Jamie more."

You: "You feel Tim doesn't understand what it is like to be a mother and work at the same time."

Mary: "If he would just help me with dinner and bedtime, I could get caught up and spend more time with Jamie."

You: "Sounds like you may need to talk with Tim."

Mary: "That's right. I've been struggling with this on my own. Thanks for helping me see that I need to talk to Tim. I know he will help me."

7. a. How did Mary arrive at her conclusion that she needs to talk to Tim?

   b. Is her problem solved? Why, or why not?

   c. How do you think active listening made her feel?

As you can see, we're a long way from "You ought to quit work" or "You ought to sell your house." By reflecting what she is saying and by continually hearing, you've let Mary talk it out and come to her own solution. This is what active listening does.

It's not your job as a friend to make sure Mary does what you think is wisest or most ethical. If she asks for your advice, you might offer the pros and cons of the options as you see them. But telling her what to do is unlikely to encourage her long-term spiritual maturity or make her feel loved. However, if Mary were obviously making a moral decision contrary to scriptural teaching, a kind word of warning concerning God's written boundaries for right living would be in order.

LET'S GET PERSONAL

8. How do you feel about learning to listen to others in this way?

9. Think of one of your relationships that could be improved if you followed the principle in James 1:19 that everyone should be quick to listen and slow to speak. Write down that person's name.

As an assignment for next week, memorize Proverbs 18:13: "He who answers before listening—that is his folly and his shame." Write this verse on an index card and review it at least three times a day this week.

Pray that the Lord will give you a caring heart to listen to others without a spirit of judgment. Ask the Lord to show you how you can express love and concern for others through active listening.

FEELING WORDS AND POSSIBLE OPENERS FOR ACTIVE LISTENING

abandoned	displeased	isolated	serene
abused	distant	jealous	shaky
afraid	doubtful	joyful	shocked
alarmed	dreary	lonely	shy
alienated	ecstatic	longing	sorrowful
amazed	elated	loving	surprised
ambivalent	embarrassed	low	suspicious
angry	empty	misunderstood	tense
annoyed	excited	needed	terrified
anxious	exhausted	neglected	threatened
apprehensive	fearful	nervous	timid
bitter	flustered	obligated	tired
bored	frightened	offended	torn
calm	frustrated	overwhelmed	uncertain
cheerful	furious	panicky	undecided
comfortable	glad	peaceful	uneasy
compassionate	gloomy	pleased	unloved
concerned	grateful	pressured	unsure
confused	grieved	proud	upset
crushed	guilty	punished	used
defeated	happy	puzzled	useful
defensive	hateful	rejected	useless
dejected	helpless	reluctant	vengeful
delighted	hesitant	resentful	warm
depressed	hopeless	responsible	weak
deserted	horrified	revengeful	weary
desperate	hurt	sad	withdrawn
despondent	inadequate	satisfied	wonderful
discouraged	insecure	scared	worn out
disgusted	irritated	secure	

You seem to be . . .   You sound . . .   You're saying that . . .
Seems as though . . .   Sounds like . . .   I'm hearing you say . . .

Common Hindrances to Caring Responses

From a bystander's point of view, I am sure I looked like an efficient, color-coordinated professional as I boarded a plane in Minneapolis. But beneath the surface, I was in turmoil, experiencing the first stages of grief.

While buckling my seat belt, I made the usual courteous comments to the young executive next to me. As the flight progressed we chatted informally, and the young man asked me why I was going to Atlanta. With a lump in my throat and a broken voice I answered, "My daughter miscarried our first grandchild, and I want to get there as soon as possible."

It was immediately evident that this kind man had not had any classes in active listening. His response to me was, "Oh, my wife just found out she is pregnant." I knew he was trying to be helpful by staying on the same subject, but he ignored my feelings and the message I had just sent. He did not reflect them back to me. To reiterate the metaphor of the tennis game in session 3, he did not return my serve but hit his own ball instead.

I remember wishing I had never said anything about my situation. Talking about it had resurfaced my pain, and I got involved in a conversation about his wife, his children, and his job. Has this ever happened to you?

1. Think of a time when you wanted to be heard, but the message you sent was ignored. Share that experience with one person next to you.

FOUR POTENTIAL HINDRANCES

In this session we will look at some common hindrances to being active listeners who can give caring responses. The young executive struggled with one.

Telling Your Own Story
It is very common to listen to someone else and suddenly hook into a memory out of our own experience. At that point, many of us are prone to take the focus away from the person speaking and put it on ourselves by relating a similar story or event. The hurting person feels ignored or discounted because the conversation now is centered on our experience instead of the message he or she needs to express.

Let's look at how this can happen in conversation.

David: "I just learned that my father has cancer."

Rick: "Oh, my mother had cancer last year. She had surgery and is just doing great."

It is easy to think that telling a happy-ending story is what the hurting person needs. Happy-ending stories are encouraging, but *first* acknowledge how the person is hurting at the moment. Listen to his or her story, respond appropriately, then later tell your wonderful story.

Being Uncomfortable With Another's Pain
In a culture geared to the pleasure principle, it is unpleasant to welcome pain into our lives. Many of us have not been taught to acknowledge our own feelings. Instead, we go to great lengths to keep life on an intellectual, logical basis.

However, when a person experiences a great loss or crisis, logic and reasoning and someone else's experience fall short in mediating his deep feelings of sadness and grief. The logical caregiver can seem cold and calculating, ready to dispense easy solutions or minimize hurt. As I mentioned in session 1, the hurting person needs to be comforted with understanding and acceptance. This can be accomplished with empathic, reflective statements.

If the young executive on the plane had said, "This is a difficult trip for you," or "You seem very sad," I would have felt understood. If he had been comfortable with my pain, I could have talked some more and possibly felt some relief of my pain, which I had bottled up and controlled during the rush of canceling appointments and preparing for the trip.

Learning to be comfortable with someone else's pain is a key to staying with him or her through those difficult situations that have no easy solutions.

2. Now investigate some Scripture passages that encourage us to develop this capacity for caring. The group can divide into triads, with each triad choosing one of the Scriptures below. It may be necessary for some triads to cover two passages, so that each passage is considered.

Proverbs 15:23   Philippians 2:3-4
Proverbs 25:11   Colossians 3:12-13
Romans 15:1-2

   After reading your passage, finish the following sentence. This verse is telling me that I should . . .

3. Each triad should read its sentence(s) aloud to the rest of the group.

4. How would you summarize the common message of these passages?

Needing to Fix
This is a third hindrance to active listening.

In my private practice I was working with a young

woman experiencing severe depression. As I questioned her about her support system, I asked her if she had contacted her mother, who lived in another city. She immediately answered, "Oh, no, I could never tell her. She would only give me advice and quote Bible verses, and I can't handle that right now."

The inclination to give advice when someone is hurting comes from a sincere desire to help. But it is not always "help" that is helpful. Many times we endeavor to fix so that *we* will be more comfortable and not have to face the feelings of someone in pain.

Suggestions are beneficial when the hurting person asks for them, but advice that sounds like a command intended to control the person or a demand usually results in defensiveness. To receive advice, one must first feel understood and accepted. We are called to be *caregivers,* not *curegivers.*

5. Read 1 Corinthians 3:6-9. It further explains this concept.

   a. Who is to plant and water?   *We*

   b. Who gives the increase?   *God*

   c. What are the implications for caregiving?   —
   I Only . . . .
   guilt . . . .

Making Assumptions and Judgments

A friend of mine lost a loved one whose lifestyle had been filled with unwise choices. A woman who knew my friend only as a pastor's wife and was not close to her family wrote her a note: "It must be such a comfort to know that your sister is with the Lord."

My friend felt anger toward someone who would make such an assumption without checking out the circumstances surrounding her grief. She had no such assurance of her sister's destiny, and she was far from comforted by the woman's highlighting the subject. It is easy to make assumptions or judgments from appearances or from your own similar situation, but they can cause more hurt when you desire to help.

Hurting persons often resist reaching out for help because they fear being judged. By being critical or condemning if another person's value system is different from ours, we go against biblical instructions to build up others.

6. The Scriptures are consistent in condemning the "judging" of others (Matthew 7:1-5, Romans 14:1–15:4). But Jesus Christ and Paul also repeatedly pray for and urge believers to have discernment (Matthew 7:6, 15-20; Philippians 1:9-11). What is the difference between judging and discerning?

7. Now reconsider the illustration about Mary that appeared in session 3. Mary says to you, "I love my job, but since Jamie was born, I can't seem to keep up. I don't like taking her to childcare, but Tim says we need my income to stay in our new home."

   a. What possible judgments may hinder you from listening to Mary?

   b. If you express these judgments to her, how do you think they will affect your relationship with her?

   c. What if Mary makes a decision you think is unbiblical because you gave her no advice?

    d. Explain some ways to overcome making assumptions
       and judgments when listening to people or hearing
       about someone's circumstances.

Listen first

WHAT THE BIBLE SAYS ABOUT THESE HINDRANCES

The Bible portrays friends who tried to help someone in a
terrible situation with no easy answers.

    8. Job was a godly man who had lost his children, wealth,
       and health in a series of tragedies. Job's friends offered
       him a lot of advice. In triads, choose one passage—Job
       4:7-11, 8:4-7, or 15:5-6—and answer the following ques-
       tions.

       a. Summarize what the friend is basically saying.

       b. Was this friend's "help" helpful? Why, or why not?

       c. Are there any suggestions you would like to convey to
          him about active listening and caring responses? What
          are they?

    9. Now read Job's response in Job 16:2-5. What can you
       learn about helping from his reply?

(1) *Don't judge when you don't know circumstances*

(2) *Acknowledge his pain*

(3) *Help where you can*

(4) *Listen to all he says · look beyond*

LET'S GET PERSONAL

10. Now the group should divide into pairs—a speaker and a listener. Someone can set a timer for two minutes. The speaker is to talk for two minutes without any interruptions or comments. At the end of two minutes the listener should respond with "You seem to be feeling _____ because_____."
    Now reverse roles and repeat the exercise.

11. a. How did it feel to listen for two minutes without responding?

    b. How did it feel to be listened to for two minutes uninterrupted?

In closing as a group, four volunteers can read aloud the following passages of Scripture from Proverbs. After the group reading, have a time of prayer.

> The tongue of the wise commends knowledge,
>   but the mouth of the fool gushes folly. (15:2)

> A man finds joy in giving an apt reply—
>   and how good is a timely word! (15:23)

> A word aptly spoken is
>   like apples of gold in settings of silver. (25:11)

> Do you see a man who speaks in haste?
>   There is more hope for a fool than for him. (29:20)

As an assignment for next week, review the verses in this session and commit one of them to memory.
    Determine to listen actively to three people this week. Write down how you felt about it and how the other person responded.

Without Wearing

Be Gentle With Yourself

She drove eighty miles to keep her appointment with me. Shirley was very concerned and wanted to know the best way to help her neighbor.

Shirley and Pat had moved into the same neighborhood five years ago. Shirley had befriended Pat, and they shared many good times together. Through the years, however, Pat had many emotional upheavals, marital difficulties, and personal disappointments. Shirley tried to be there for Pat. She took her places, baby-sat for her, provided meals for the family, and listened by the hour to Pat talking about her pain and confusion. But the situation was not improving. In fact, things were getting worse.

With tears in her eyes, Shirley told me that she was falling apart trying to care for Pat. Her own family life was tense. She was apprehensive every time the phone rang or there was a knock at the door. She feared the rage of Pat's husband who was threatening divorce and desertion. Pat was making inappropriate demands of Shirley, using suicide as a threat when Shirley would not cooperate. Shirley felt her only way out was to sell her house and move.

As I listened to Shirley, it became clear that she had lost herself while helping another. I remembered some people I had tried to help so many times, but my efforts had resulted in the same tension. I empathized deeply with Shirley's questions: "What does God expect of me as a Christian and a caring person?" "Why am I experiencing so much frustration when my desire is to be obedient to God's command to share another's burden?" These are familiar questions for people who care.

In the previous sessions, you have learned about how to care: ways to offer help to hurting people and the importance of being a good listener. For the next four sessions we'll look at caring without wearing. In this session the focus will be on some of the reasons caring people experience burnout and disappointment when reaching out to others.

   1. Can you think of a specific time when you felt overwhelmed or unsure when caring for someone?
      Three or four people may want to share their answers with the group.

FIVE UNREALISTIC EXPECTATIONS

During our session, I affirmed Shirley's desire to care for Pat and began to explore with her five unrealistic expectations that hinder efforts to care. As we talked, I could visibly see Shirley relax.

I have the ability to change another person.
Coming to grips with the reality that, no matter what I say or do, I have no power to change another person gives me a relaxing perspective on caring. I can suggest change, but the other person must choose to change himself or herself. It is difficult to accept the fact that *I* am the only person I can change. This insight helps me to focus on caring rather than working toward a cure. It also frees me to assist the other person to follow his or her own course rather than the one I feel is best.

Remember the rich young ruler who asked Christ what he should do? Although Jesus responded with the perfect answer to his problem, the young man chose to go his own way (Mark 10:17-22).

I have the capacity to help everyone.
Being sensitive to someone's need came naturally for me. I
was the oldest of three daughters, and assisting someone
and trying to relieve his or her pain always seemed like the
most appropriate response. But many times I recognize that
I want to relieve someone else's pain just so I can feel more
comfortable. Or I feel more comfortable focusing on another's
pain rather than looking at my own needs.

Elisa Morgan in her radio program "Considerations"
calls this kind of helping "rescuing." She defines it as taking
responsibility for other people and their problems to the point
of caretaking and people pleasing. It is a very unhealthy way
of relating to others.

There should never be any limits to what I can do.
When I was younger, I believed that setting limits was being
selfish. If someone was in need and wanted to talk on the
phone for long periods of time, I felt it would be selfish to
limit the call or call back at a more convenient time. The out-
come of this thinking is feeling powerless and angry, which
gets in the way of loving and listening.

I am the only person available to help.
This expectation also leads to unhealthy helping because it
brings with it a sense of being trapped. My self-pity escalates
when I perceive I am the only one who cares. On the other
hand, this expectation also feeds my need to feel special,
giving me a false sense of self-worth.

I must never make a mistake.
Being right and doing right are built-in desires from child-
hood. Donald Sloat says it well in his book *The Dangers of
Growing Up in a Christian Home*:

> Somehow the notion that perfect is better seems to have
> found a place in our lives and in our churches, because
> there seems to be something about human nature that
> believes being perfect is going to result in love and
> acceptance, whereas open admission of weakness invites

criticism and rejection. Thus to many of us, the admonitions toward perfection are attractive because we want to gain love and avoid rejection.[1]

Our fear of failure and the rejection we would then incur motivate us to try to control an environment and the behavior of others around us.

The major difficulty with all of these expectations is that they lead to burnout in caring. Each expectation is partially caused by our self-centeredness because it is connected to our performance and personal power to effect change. This is the opposite of what God really expects from us.

At this point, your large group should divide into subgroups of two or three persons to discuss answers to questions 2 through 5.

2. How do these unrealistic expectations reflect self-centeredness?

3. Do you think any of these beliefs have been influencing your actions and feelings? If so, how?

4. How would rejecting these expectations affect your life?

5. What biblical truths have been distorted into these expectations?

Gal. 6:9 & 10.

Also ask for wisdom

Trust in the Lord..

Led by the Spirit

SOMETIMES WE CAN CARE TOO MUCH

6. Read Exodus 18:13-26 aloud. These verses portray a
   caring leader trying to meet the needs of his people.

   a. How would you characterize what Moses was doing for
      his people?

   b. Identify Moses' expectations of himself.

   Heavy responsibility

   c. Why do you think his father-in-law questioned him?

   Felt Moses was handling too much.
   & was concerned.

   d. How did Moses respond?

   Stop & thought what he was
   doing & also what Jethro had said

   e. What was Jethro's greatest concern for Moses (verses
      17-18)? *That he would wear himself*
      off

   f. Consider the alternative Jethro suggested for caring
      for the people. How did it go to the root of Moses'
      situation? *Lifted the load* *Ask f wisdom*

   Gal - 6:9 & 10

A REALISTIC APPROACH

I can almost hear Jethro saying, "Moses, things are heavy
around here. You have a lot to carry, leading these people and
caring for them. Be gentle with yourself. Let's take a look at
what you can do and what you cannot do."

   Suppose that Moses and Jethro took a sheet of paper and
made two columns:

WHAT I CAN DO	WHAT I CANNOT DO
Get some more people to help.	I cannot do it all alone.
Be a listener.	Make everyone happy.
Set specific times to be available.	Go without sleep.
Delegate responsibilities.	

Next think about what Shirley can realistically expect of herself:

WHAT I CAN DO	WHAT I CANNOT DO
Be a listener.	Change Pat.
Set specific times to be available.	Cure her hurts.
Stay objective.	Alter her family relationships.
Pray for Pat regularly.	
Report her talk of suicide to other family members.	
Suggest professional help.	
Seek guidance for myself.	

A helpful phrase to remember when you experience the frustration of caring in a situation with no easy answers is, *Be gentle with yourself.*

LET'S GET PERSONAL

7. Do you have a present situation that is overwhelming or frustrating you? On your own, briefly describe that situation.

8. Now be gentle with yourself and fill out the following chart on your own.

WHAT I CAN DO	WHAT I CANNOT DO

9. Share your situation and chart with two other group members.

10. Does this represent any changes you need to make in the way you are caring for someone? If so, what change do you want to make this week? Tell your two partners.

In closing this session, spend time in your triad praying for each person. Pray that God will give you each the insight and courage to change what needs to be changed, and trust Him for His power to cure while you remain faithful to care.

Unrealistic

① Only one · never make mistake
②

Reaching Out
Within Your Limits

T he doctor told me, "Go immediately to the hospital." I wanted to argue with him and say, "It isn't that bad," but deep inside I knew. I knew I was at the end of my rope.

Lying in my hospital bed on New Year's Eve, hearing the sounds of the world celebrating a new year, I felt frustrated. The same thoughts kept running through my mind: *How did I get here? Why the physical problems? Thyroid disease! What does that mean? I'm so young! My family needs me! This isn't fair!*

When I received the news that I was facing a one-year recovery period, I was furious that my lifestyle would be interrupted. As a mother of young children, pastor's wife, substitute teacher in the public school, choir member, teacher training instructor, and hostess of many meetings, among other things, I could not believe this was happening to me.

Dealing with my physical burnout, I began to understand for the first time how my life source was based on performance and caretaking in hopes of gaining love and acceptance. I was addicted to doing for others but spent very little energy doing for myself. Doing for others permitted me to keep my feelings of inadequacy and low self-esteem undercover. I did not know how to face the pain of the past or the present. The concept of self-care seemed so selfish.

In the process of recovering from that crisis, I learned that the opposite of burnout is balance. Learning how to reach out within my limits requires understanding who I am, acknowledging who God is, having realistic expectations of myself, and adopting a lifestyle that gives priority to abiding in God's love, wisdom, and daily guidance. That is the key to caring without wearing out.

In the previous sessions we have considered ways to show that we are God's disciples by being sensitive to people's needs, listening actively, expressing care, and recognizing our role as caregivers, not curegivers. In this session we concentrate on listening to ourselves, accepting the reality that burden bearing is stressful and requires continual support to keep our lives in balance.

Burnout is not an uncommon problem—even in ministry. In their book *Love Is a Choice,* authors Robert Hemfelt, Frank Minirth, and Paul Meier write,

> At the clinic we see many Christian workers who have just come in from the field, domestic fields as well as foreign missions. You can almost see the pain and weariness on their faces. But should we tell them "Look: If you hope to serve others you must first take care of yourself," big neon lights flash on. Selfish! Selfish! A good Christian worker puts self aside. Selfishness is a sin.[1]

The entire group can begin this session by discussing the following two questions.

1. When you hear the term *self-care,* what comes to your mind?

2. When you hear the word *burnout,* what do you think about?

A WEARY WORKER

Moses was one biblical caregiver who was burning out in his ministry. We can learn from his experience.

3. Read Numbers 11:10-15.

   a. What was Moses asking God about?

   b. How do you think Moses was feeling?

   frustrated inadequate depressed,

   c. What did he see as his alternatives? *Vse 15*

4. Have you ever had similar feelings in a leadership or caregiving situation? What do you tend to wail about?

5. Now read Numbers 11:16-17 to discover God's answer to Moses.

   a. What does God promise Moses?

   Spiritual help by bringing others along side.

   b. How is this promise like or unlike what you need?

6. Each person in the group can look up one of the following passages. Four volunteers can explain what these passages say about how our need for support is satisfied.

   Psalm 34:17-19   Hebrews 4:15-16
   Isaiah 40:31   Hebrews 10:24-25

7. How could doing these things prevent burnout?

YOUR CURRENT NEED FOR SUPPORT

As she filled the bottles with formula and listened to the churning of the washing machine, Ruth recalled the days when she dressed in a business suit and made her way downtown to the bank. She thought of doing volunteer work at the nursing home, editing the church newsletter, and being care coordinator for her Sunday school class.

How different things had been since the arrival of the twins! Her overwhelming joy with God's precious gifts of life to her was mixed with chronic fatigue, and at times she felt hopeless that she would ever do anything again beyond the changing table and the rocking chair.

Her world seemed so small. There was no time to reach out to others, no time for phone calls to friends. Although she was busy, she felt isolated and lonely. Ruth realized that *she needed care.*

The changing seasons and circumstances of life bring with them varying degrees of needing care and giving care. Ecclesiastes 3:1 declares, "There is a time for everything, and a season for every activity under heaven." This is true for caring for self as well as caring for others.

LET'S GET PERSONAL

8. The following exercise will assist you in assessing your present circumstances and personal need for support.

   a. Circle the season of your life.

   Pre-Adulthood (17-22)   Middle Adulthood (36-55)
   Early Adulthood (23-35)   Later Adulthood (over 55)

b. Underline your family structure.

Single with others   Married with children
Single with children   Married without children
Single and independent Married with blended family

c. Circle the number of people you feel responsibility for daily.

(1) 2 3 4 5 6 7 8 9 10   more than 10

d. Circle your present stress level.

LOW	MEDIUM	HIGH
Sense of calm	Dealing with	Dealing with crises
Routine established	transition	High anxiety
High satisfaction	Daily struggles	Burnout
with life	Many unfinished	
	tasks	

After finishing the exercise, find someone in the group who has at least two similarities to your circumstances. Allow three to five minutes per person so that both of you can talk about your current situations. Then complete question 9 and discuss your answers together.

9. a. Right now, what are you feeling about your present life situation?

At Ease Hopeful Frustrated Overwhelmed Other (specify)

b. Identify some special challenges of this season of your life.

c. Give examples of things you enjoy about this season of your life.

d. What are some of your opportunities for caring?

e. How would you characterize your particular needs for self-care? Do you feel you need more emotional support, physical support, or spiritual support?

Close in prayer with your partner. Pray specifically about the challenges and opportunities he or she faces in his or her season of life.

Ask the Lord to help you appreciate your own season of life and sense the multitude of opportunities for caring.

Be realistic about your current level of stress, and be gentle with yourself about the need for emotional, physical, and spiritual support.

Wearing and Warning Signs

T he brochure taped on my refrigerator door announced the upcoming stress management seminar to be held next Saturday morning at a local university. I was a full-time mother, a full-time pastor's wife, a full-time director of Christian education, and a no-time person. My biggest clue that I should attend was that I felt there was no time to spare to spend three hours finding out about stress management. But since I felt like I was living in a wind tunnel with an exhaust fan, I decided to go.

The first assignment I was given in the seminar was to take a piece of newsprint, get on the floor with a box of crayons—along with all the other sophisticated professionals who were looking for answers to life—and draw a map of my world.

We were instructed to draw various-sized boxes or circles to represent all of our present involvements in activities and relationships. The next step was to color the map using a red crayon to indicate which activities and relationships represented stress and a green crayon to indicate support. Figure A on the following page shows my drawing (most of it was in red, indicating a high degree of stress). The S's represent staff and the C's represent coordinators I worked with as Christian education director.

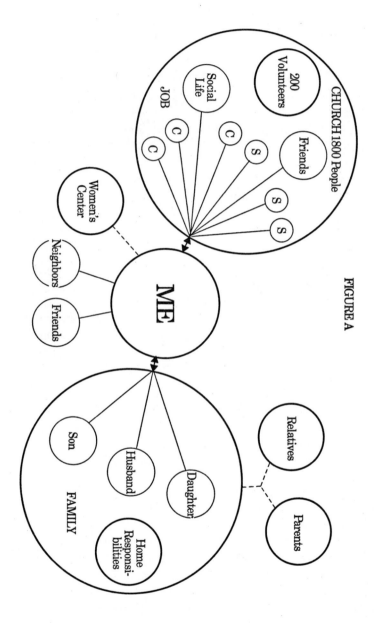

FIGURE A

That exercise changed my life. I came face-to-face with a graphic picture of the way I was feeling. While coloring my activities and relationships, I soon realized I was living in a vise, pressured by all the "good" I was doing. I also became aware of the picture's imbalance. My stress level far exceeded my support level.

I went home that day knowing I was near another breaking point. Although I claimed that Christ was the center of my life, and I was reading my Bible and praying, something was missing. I wrote a little note to myself on my paper, "Carol, how did you get here again? Something has to change."

Gleaning more information from the seminar, I recognized that stress management was nothing more than self-management. My first step to change was to take responsibility for my present condition and to own the consequences of my daily choices. I acknowledged that I had not respected my limits. I knew I needed a system for evaluating my choices. I needed someone to be accountable to and talk to about why I was doing what I was doing.

In this session we will continue to look at our need for self-care and how that relates to communing with God and developing an intimate relationship with Him.

1. The following internal messages can drive us beyond our limits. Circle the one(s) that you struggle with at times.

   ♦ I never seem to be doing enough.
   ♦ I am responsible for changing another person.
   ♦ It is selfish to take care of myself.

   Tell the group your answers and explain where you learned that message.

JESUS MODELS SELF-CARE

2. Read Mark 6:45-46 and Luke 5:15-16. Consider what Christ did after a long day of training His disciples, teaching, and doing miracles.

a. How did Jesus take care of Himself? What did self-care involve?

Prayed - sought solitude rested + pondered.

b. What do you think He prayed about?

strength, direction, discernment + wisdom. certain people.

c. Do you think others were ever displeased with Him because He left the crowds to spend time alone in prayer? If so, why do you think they would be displeased? *They loved Him so*

d. At what point do you think He knew it was imperative to withdraw from the crowd and be alone with His Father?

WE NEED DIRECTION

Holding my eight-month-old grandson in my arms was an exercise in "touch management." David's energetic, curious interest in touching, pulling, feeling, and shaking everything he saw kept me busy. Because of my love for him, I wanted him to enjoy his world. At the same time I wanted to keep him safe. I thought, *How like my heavenly Father who longs to hold me in His everlasting arms and guide my choices because of His great love for me.*

David the psalmist knew the importance of this daily guidance when he said, "In the morning, O LORD, you hear my voice; in the morning I lay my requests before you and wait in expectation" (Psalm 5:3).

3. Different group members can look up each of the following verses. Then each person can report the benefits his

or her passage promises to us if we make time alone with our heavenly Father, to read His Word and commune with Him in prayer, a priority in our lives.

Psalm 18:3	Psalm 73:23-24
Psalm 25:14-15	2 Corinthians 1:3-4
Psalm 32:8	Philippians 4:6-7
Psalm 34:5	Hebrews 4:16 *With confidence*
Psalm 37:4-5	

4. a. Most of us know there are many benefits to a consistent prayer life. But what are some common hindrances that keep us from this basic step in self-care?

Not understanding our position before God. Interruptions.

b. Are there people in your life or activities demanding your time and attention that keep you from being alone with God on a daily basis? If so, what needs to change for you to maintain regular spiritual support?

More discipline

COMMON WEARING AND WARNING SIGNS

The following list of warning signs indicates my life is out of balance and self-care needs to be adjusted.

♦ When I am irritable and short with the people I love the most.
♦ When my quiet time is rushed and my attitude is, "Well, I've done that."
♦ When my exercise schedule is less than three hours a week.
♦ When the fruit of my spirit is to be critical and complain.

◆ When I am eating more and liking it less.
◆ When I am throwing longer pity parties and inviting more people.
◆ When I feel like nobody cares, nobody helps, and nobody loves me.
◆ When my calendar has no fun appointments.
◆ When I wish people would not ask me to do anything.
◆ When I want to just quit.

5. Why would an honest-to-goodness, compassionate, caring person ever have such feelings or behaviors?

6. Possibly Martha was feeling like this when she was busy preparing a meal for Jesus. Read Luke 10:38-42.

   a. What were Martha's wearing and warning signs?
   Irritable to people she loved not
   Feeling sorry for self

   b. What was Jesus' counsel to Martha?
   Try not to do too much, concen[tr]ate
   on what is important.

7. a. Do you identify with any of the wearing and warning signs? If so, which one(s)?

   b. How do you think Jesus would counsel you right now?

SEVEN PRINCIPLES FOR SELF-CARE

Caregivers must feel cared for.
Caregivers need a power source.
Caregivers must have proper nutrition, rest, and
    exercise.
Caregivers must learn how to be gentle with
    themselves.
Caregivers need support and encouragement.
Caregivers must respect limits and set boundaries.
Caregivers need to laugh and play.

A caregiver must feel cared for.

Spend time each day with your heavenly Father who uncon-
ditionally loves you. Martha Stout says it so well: "The more
fully we experience the gentle touch of Christ upon our
lives—loving us, forgiving us, healing us—the more gentle we
will become with each other."[1]

Many books and guides set forth recommendations
for spending time with God, but the bigger issue seems
to be valuing yourself enough to make the time or truly
believing that doing this is important to you and your
well-being.

A caregiver needs a power source.

Caring for others—responding to their physical and emotional needs—requires strength, energy, patience, and
wisdom. John 15:5 makes it clear that "apart from me [God]
you can do nothing." Recognize your dependence on God
for wisdom and strength to do your part as an effective
caregiver.

A caregiver must have proper nutrition, rest, and exercise.

An adequate, balanced diet plays a big role in physical
health. Eating foods loaded with sugar can cause giant mood
swings. Failing to eat on a regular schedule can diminish the
body's natural immune system. Plenty of rest means more
than just the hours you sleep at night. You need regular time

away from all the demands placed on you. A brisk walk can do wonders to revive both body and spirit.

Be gentle with yourself.
Remind yourself that caring for others is stressful. If you are helping someone with his grief, your own unresolved grief experiences may be brought to the surface. You may struggle with finding the appropriate response and feel helpless at times. Allow yourself to be human, and learn how to acknowledge the value of the help you give. If you truly listen from your heart, you give a priceless gift.

A caregiver needs a supportive group.
Meeting your own social and emotional needs is essential to being effective when caring for others. The plant that is watered and fertilized yields the best fruit. Being part of a support group enables you to share your joy and struggles, be encouraged by others, and seek God's power through prayer. Your support system may be just one person who listens to you, or you may want to form a support group. (See "Suggested Prayer Support Group Format.")

Respect your limits and exercise your power of choice.
Being in control rather than being controlled by your circumstances is a true measure of self-care. Everyone is limited by energy, resources, money, time, and ability. Define what others can expect from you. Knowing your limits and adjusting your world to respect what you can and cannot do prevent burnout.

A caregiver needs to laugh and play!
Medical science is discovering the benefits of laughter and rest for alleviating stress. Anticipated regular "time-outs" for enjoyable activities provide a change of pace and contribute to more balanced living.

LET'S GET PERSONAL

8. Now, make an assessment. On a scale of 1 to 10, measure your level of self-care by circling the appropriate number.

	POOR CARE					VERY GOOD CARE			
Maintaining Intimate Relation- ship With God	1 2 ③ 4 5 6 7 8 9 10
Pursuing Healthy Habits	1 2 3 ④⑤⑥ 7 8 9 10
Being Gentle With Myself	1 2 3 4 ⑤ 6 7 8 9 10
Sharing Within Support System	1 2 3 4 5 6 ⑦ 8 9 10
Respecting Limits	1 2 ③ 4 5 6 7 8 9 10
Laughing and Playing	1 2 3 4 ⑤ 6 7 8 9 10

9. Finish this sentence: Right now I recognize an area of self-care that needs attention is . . .

\# 1   *More time spent with God & the Word.*
Respecting limits

Tell your answer to the group.

10. As you reflect on this session and your assessment of self-care, do you feel a need to make any changes in your lifestyle? Explain.

yes — limiting myself — I have a tendancy to spread myself too thin.

Have a time of prayer to close the session.

11. At home this week, set aside time to draw a map of your world. (You may want to use one of the blank pages at the end of this guide.) Use circles or squares to represent the people and activities in your life. Draw strong connecting lines to show persons and activities that demand major attention, and use lighter lines to indicate lesser involvement.

Think of the degrees of stress and support in your life. Color your map with red to represent stress and green to represent support. Some involvements will represent both.

After drawing your map, answer the following questions.

a. What do I think others expect of me?

b. What expectations do I place on myself?

c. What do I think God expects of me?

In the next session, you will have an opportunity to share your map with the members of your group.

Figure A on page 64 reflects my out-of-balance former life. Figure B shows my present, more balanced situation. If you could see it in color, you would find a lot less red and more green.

FIGURE B

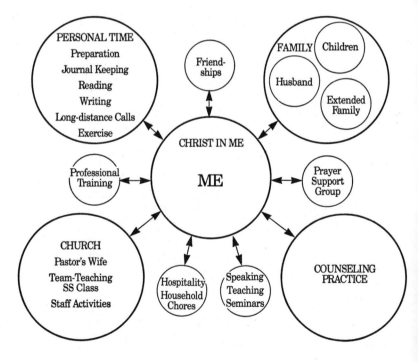

Keeping the Balance

After opening in prayer, take one minute each to share the map of your world. Tell the group briefly what you learned from doing this exercise.

Using the following case study, let's review the principles of caring without wearing.

Judy and Ron Daniels are active members of a local evangelical church. Ron is completing a graduate degree in evening school. He and Judy have three sons, ages six years, three years, and five months. Ron also has sole responsibility for his grandfather in a nearby nursing home.

Judy has continually struggled with intense anxiety and a fear of dying at an early age. Judy's doctor recently informed her that surgery was needed to remove a recurrent benign tumor in her neck and throat. Doing so would require extensive work on her face and splitting her jawbone, leaving her face partially paralyzed. Her speech would also be affected, and she would have to pursue a demanding follow-up program of speech and physical therapy.

In this last session we will explore ways of caring for the Daniels family at their time of need.

Keep in mind these three principles about giving help that is helpful. First, we are caregivers, not curegivers. Second, active listening is imperative to helping relationships.

Third, hurting people need assurance of support.

1. The first thing to do is to *make an assessment.* Imagine
   that you know the Daniels family. Fill in the following
   chart about them and you, taking into consideration your
   season of life, present demands, gifts, abilities, and wearing and warning signs. (You may want to refer to the list
   of ways to express caring on page 25 in session 2.)

JUDY'S NEEDS	RON'S NEEDS	CHILDREN'S NEEDS

WHAT I CAN DO	WHAT I CANNOT DO

Your group can break up into smaller groups of four or five
persons, and discuss what you wrote in this assessment.

2. Next, on your own, complete the following sentence. One
   way I could help the Daniels family is . . .

3. In the larger group, each person can take this opportunity to read aloud his or her completed sentence.

Jim is a friend of the Daniels family. While helping them and managing his own daily demands, Jim receives word that his mother has become seriously ill. The same day his son comes home from school with an F grade in two subjects. And at work a team member tells him that her husband wants out of their marriage.

4. a. How do you think Jim is feeling?

   b. What do you believe Jim needs?

5. Turn to Numbers 11:10-23, which you read in session 6. What similarities do you see between Moses and Jim?

6. Identify Moses' wearing and warning signs (see pages 67-68 in session 7).

When he confessed that the burden was too heavy for him to bear, Moses took three steps.

  Step One: He acknowledged his feelings of power-
       lessness.
  Step Two: He recognized God as His source of power
       and wisdom.
  Step Three: He accepted the support God offered him
       and shared the burden with others.

7. Why do you suppose God didn't condemn Moses for initially being overwhelmed and angry?

8. How did God affirm that Moses could not lead those people alone?

9. How do you think Moses felt after talking this over with God and hearing His response?

10. After hearing from God, how did Moses react to the situation (Numbers 11:21-22)?

11. What was the meaning of God's answer to Moses (Numbers 11:23)?

12. If Jim wishes to follow Moses' example, what does he need to do?

LET'S GET PERSONAL

We've seen the need for tender care and support that Paul talks about in 1 Thessalonians 2:11-12: "We dealt with each of you as a father deals with his own children, encouraging,

comforting and urging you to live lives worthy of God, who
calls you into his kingdom and glory."

We've also seen our need for self-care. Being gentle
with ourselves in this day of stressful lifestyles is essential
to being gracious caregivers. I have tried to make clear that
our ultimate need is to have an intimate relationship with
Jesus Christ, which is developed by spending time together,
hearing His voice of care, comfort, instruction, and wisdom.
As we know Him and His character and discover more about
ourselves—our giftedness, uniqueness, and calling in each
season of life—we are empowered to make daily choices in
keeping with His will for our lives.

Since your time together as a group is coming to a close,
you may want to use these goals as guides for your next steps
in learning about caring without wearing.

♦ Further explore the development of an intimate relationship with Jesus Christ and set aside specific times to
be with Him.
♦ Become more skilled in active listening by practicing
and by reading more on communication skills.
♦ Begin to write down on a regular basis what I can do
and what I cannot do.
♦ Make a list of my own wearing and warning signs and
read them once a week.
♦ Pray about any new request or pressing need before
making a decision to be involved.
♦ Ask someone (or several people) to participate with me
in an ongoing prayer support group.

13. Take a couple of minutes to reflect prayerfully on these
goals. Circle the one that is appropriate for you or write
your own. In the space below write a prayer asking the
Lord Jesus to assist you with the realization of this goal.

Read your goal aloud to your group. Spend time praying together for yourself and the others in your group.

My prayer for each of you is found in 2 Thessalonians 2:16-17: "May our Lord Jesus Christ himself and God our Father, who loved us and by his grace gave us eternal encouragement and good hope, encourage your hearts and strengthen you in every good deed and word."

Epilogue

The phone rang as Helen came in the door from church, carrying all the toys and linens from the nursery that needed to be washed.

She did not recognize the voice at first, but Irene reminded her that they had met two weeks ago in Sunday school class. Irene had just moved from Omaha. She wanted to know if Helen could possibly meet her on Thursday for lunch.

Helen remembered the conversation with Irene and really empathized with how hard it was to move, leaving familiar surroundings and feeling lost and lonely in a new city. However, as she heard Irene's request, Helen's stomach started to knot.

There was nothing she would rather do, but she had been recognizing lately that she never had time for prayer, reflection, Bible reading, and just enjoying a good book. As a result of trying to make some changes, she had finally worked out a co-op baby-sitting program that gave her Thursday mornings free for some self-care time.

While still on the phone, she remembered the first step in her new program was not to make impulse decisions, so she responded to Irene by saying, "Let me look at my schedule, and I'll get back to you."

After she hung up, her real struggle began. She had a long conversation with herself. "How can I say no to someone who is so lonely and doesn't know anyone?" "I do have some free time to go to lunch now that I have the co-op." "Wouldn't it be selfish to spend that time alone reading?" "What kind of testimony would I be giving if I said no?" "I should at least be able to do that for someone new in town."

But deep inside Helen knew that if she continued the pace of the last two months, serving on the nursery committee, parenting two preschool children, working part-time in her home, and sharing the responsibilities with her husband in their growth group, without taking any time for renewal, she would continue to be irritable and frustrated with her continual daily demands.

Helen started to pray as she prepared lunch. She told the Lord that it wasn't an attitude of helpfulness she lacked, but it was so hard to set aside time for herself. It just did not feel right with all the pressing needs facing her. As she prayed, a thought came to her. She could call Irene and let her know that Thursday was not a convenient day to have lunch but that she would love to invite her to their growth group on Tuesday evening. If that did not work out, she could see her at the women's Bible study that meets every other Wednesday morning at the church.

Helen's sense of relief in keeping her appointment with God on Thursday morning made the struggle worthwhile. She knew that learning to care without wearing was a new approach to life for her. She would need ongoing wisdom with daily choices as she worked to balance demands, discipline her time, and appreciate the importance of self-care. But she had learned that sometimes she could say yes without adding more to her schedule. Helen had begun to learn about balance, and like you, she would be better at caring without wearing.

Guidelines
for Group Leaders

Small group studies have many benefits. First, educators
agree that content is best communicated in print or lecture,
whereas skills and attitudes are best acquired in group inter-
action. But even more in a study about caring, a small group
offers the chance to give and receive care in a supportive setting. Your aim as a leader is to provide an environment that
helps people know and feel comfortable with one another.
The questions in this guide have been designed to make this
task easier.

Develop a genuine interest in each person's remarks, and
expect members of the group to learn from one another. Show
you care by listening carefully. Be affirming and open to all
responses.

Your style of leadership will depend on the size of your
group and whether the group will do homework. If participants answer questions before meeting, your role will be to
facilitate a discussion of prepared answers either in a large
group (more than six to eight persons) or in small subgroups
(two to four persons). If the participants use meeting time
to look up Scripture texts and fill in the answers, they will
have less time to process answers. However, the sessions are
designed so that you can cover them in ninety minutes without homework.

As the leader, you will be responsible to allocate time for each section of the material and allow time for closing comments and prayer. If your group is larger than eight people, you can manage time by using subgroups that discuss the topics and then report back to the larger group. The sessions have suggestions for how to do this.

Recommended meeting time is ninety minutes. If your time is shorter, you may want to consider covering the material in more than eight sessions; if your time is longer, there will be more time for processing the material and spending time in prayer as a group.

SOME SUGGESTED GROUP GUIDELINES

Review these guidelines with the group during the first session.

Maintain Confidentiality.
No one should repeat what someone shares in the group unless that person gives express permission. Even then, discretion is imperative. Be trustworthy.

Emphasize Attendance.
Each session builds on the previous ones. So, ask group members to commit to attending all eight sessions, unless an emergency arises. Being on time for each meeting is a way of being courteous.

Encourage Participation.
This is a group study. It is important that each person participate in some way in the group. However, being allowed to "pass" is also appropriate if someone does not want to answer a specific question.

Encourage honest self-expression. Participants should talk about their feelings and experiences. Negative comments about others are not appropriate.

Offer Prayers.
Open and close each session with prayer. Ask group members to pray for you as the group leader and for one another. Pray

for an atmosphere of genuine love in the group, with each
member being honestly open to learn and change.

Enjoy Group Interaction.
Be gentle with yourself as a leader and as a participant.
There is no perfect formula for a good group. Remember
God's promise of His presence. Love Him and one another as
you study and grow together.

SESSION 1

The first session sets the tone for the others, and participants
will be checking out the group to see whether they belong
there or not. One of your chief tasks in this session will be to
help people relax and get to know one another.

Begin with prayer, then briefly introduce the study.
You could summarize or read aloud a few paragraphs of the
Preface. Explain that there will be eight sessions of ninety
minutes each (or whatever you have decided).

Go over the suggested group guidelines. As a group,
set standards for your time together. These standards could
include commitment to attend, to complete suggested homework activities, or even to prepare answers for each session
ahead of time.

Ask the group's thoughts on having prayer partners
during the study. These partners would not have to meet
together outside the group session, but they could share
requests during the week by phone. You might draw numbers
to determine who would be partners.

If your group has more than eight participants, you will
want to divide into subgroups often so that everyone can participate. These subgroups can change from week to week.

If the group has not prepared answers ahead of time,
read aloud the opening story and teaching paragraphs that
lead into the questions. Then allow a minute for each person
to answer question 1. Next ask people to pair up, and allow
the pairs five minutes to get acquainted. Then bring the
group back together to introduce partners. If more than ten
people are present, you should probably divide in half for
introductions so that question 3 doesn't take too much time.

You can cover the rest of the session as a large group or in subgroups of about six. Have someone in each subgroup read the teaching paragraphs aloud as they get to them. Give the subgroups any other specific instructions, such as how much time they have. As the leader, you may want to visit different subgroups or be part of one.

Close the session as a large group in prayer.

SESSIONS 2 THROUGH 8

The rest of the sessions closely follow the format you've established in session 1. You'll spend much of your time in either the large group or, if your large group is too large for easy sharing, a large subgroup of six to eight people. You or a subgroup participant should read stories and teaching paragraphs aloud. Then fairly often you'll divide the large group(s) into smaller subgroups—pairs or triads—to do specific tasks.

Question 1 in each session functions as a warm-up. Encourage everyone to answer it briefly rather than just two or three people answering at length. Tactfully cut short lengthy stories. When storytelling is appropriate, as in session 3, we've suggested that you divide into pairs and keep the stories to five minutes at most.

Be sensitive to the pain some participants may feel. Some may be close to burnout. You may want to plan time at the end of a session to more fully pray for and listen to someone who needs care. Also, invite group members to care for one another.

At the end of session 8, you may want to raise the possibility of an ongoing support group. Ideas for launching such a group are on pages 85-86.

Suggested Prayer Support Group Format

1. Group members agree on a regular time to meet for a two-hour sharing and prayer time. It can be on a once-a-month basis or at more frequent intervals if desired.
2. Each participant comes prepared to share with the group an update on his or her walk with the Lord and current prayer needs.
3. Leadership and place can be rotated each meeting time.
4. The length of time for meeting is divided evenly among number of group members to ensure equal participation.
5. The number of participants is determined by interest and personal preference for group size.
6. Members are encouraged to pray for one another between group meetings.
7. A prayer chain can be set up on an alphabetical basis to facilitate prayer for emergency needs.
8. A six-month trial period is suggested when beginning a new group. After that time group members evaluate their own experience in the group. They can choose to continue in the group, leave the group, or branch out and form a new group.
9. Adding to the group should be done by consensus of the

whole group and at a time when it feels appropriate for the group.
10. Keep the focus of the group on prayer and support. Suggested refreshment: beverage only.

Notes

Session 2—Why Should I Care?
1. As quoted in *You Gotta Keep Dancin'* by Tim Hansel (Elgin, IL: David C. Cook, 1985), pages 16-17.
2. Taken from the article "Between You and Me," in *Stillpoint* (Fall 1987).

Session 3—Your Most Valuable Caring Skill
1. Haddon Robinson, "On Target," *Focal Point,* a publication of Denver Seminary, vol. 9, no. 2, April-June 1989.

Session 5—Be Gentle With Yourself
1. Donald E. Sloat, *The Dangers of Growing Up in a Christian Home* (Nashville, TN: Thomas Nelson, 1986), page 280.

Session 6—Reaching Out Within Your Limits
1. Robert Hemfelt, Frank Minirth, and Paul Meier, *Love Is a Choice* (Nashville, TN: Thomas Nelson, 1989), page 167.

Session 7—Wearing and Warning Signs
1. Taken from the article "Between You and Me," in *Stillpoint* (Fall 1987).